T.I.

by C.F. Earl

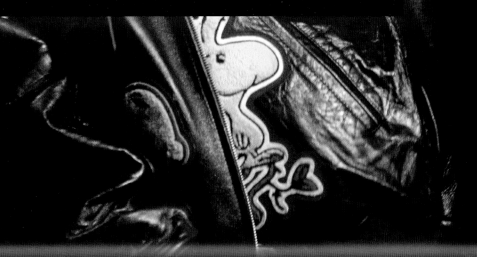

Superstars of Hip-Hop

Alicia Keys

Beyoncé

Black Eyed Peas

Ciara

Dr. Dre

Drake

Eminem

50 Cent

Flo Rida

Hip Hop:
A Short History

Jay-Z

Kanye West

Lil Wayne

LL Cool J

Ludacris

Mary J. Blige

Notorious B.I.G.

Rihanna

Sean "Diddy" Combs

Snoop Dogg

T.I.

T-Pain

Timbaland

Tupac

Usher

T.I.

by C.F. Earl

Mason Crest

T.I.

Mason Crest
370 Reed Road
Broomall, Pennsylvania 19008
www.masoncrest.com

Printed and bound in the United States of America.

First printing
9 8 7 6 5 4 3 2 1

Library of Congress Cataloging-in-Publication Data

Earl, C. F.
  T. I. / by C.F. Earl.
      p. cm. – (Superstars of hip hop)
  Includes index.
  ISBN 978-1-4222-2527-1 (hard cover) – ISBN 978-1-4222-2508-0 (series hardcover) – ISBN 978-1-4222-9229-7 (ebook)
  1. T. I. (Rapper)–Juvenile literature. 2. Rap musicians–United States–Biography–Juvenile literature. I. Title.
  ML3930.T15E27 2012
  782.421649092–dc23
  [B]
                        2011019654

Produced by Harding House Publishing Services, Inc.
www.hardinghousepages.com
Interior Design by MK Bassett-Harvey.
Cover design by Torque Advertising & Design.

Publisher's notes:
  • All quotations in this book come from original sources and contain the spelling and grammatical inconsistencies of the original text.
  • The Web sites mentioned in this book were active at the time of publication. The publisher is not responsible for Web sites that have changed their addresses or discontinued operation since the date of publication. The publisher will review and update the Web site addresses each time the book is reprinted.

DISCLAIMER: The following story has been thoroughly researched, and to the best of our knowledge, represents a true story. While every possible effort has been made to ensure accuracy, the publisher will not assume liability for damages caused by inaccuracies in the data, and makes no warranty on the accuracy of the information contained herein. This story has not been authorized nor endorsed by T.I.

Contents

Hip-Hop lingo

Rap is a kind of music where rhymes are chanted, often with music in the background. When people are **rapping**, they are making up these rhymes, sometimes off the top of their heads.

DJ is short for disc jockey. A DJ plays music on the radio or at a party and announces the songs.

A **recording studio** is a place where musicians go to record their music and turn it into CDs.

A **manager** is someone who helps and guides a musician.

An **audition** is when a person sings or performs for someone to see if that person likes his work and wants to give him a job.

A **label** is a company that produces music and sells CDs.

An **imprint** is a company that is organized as part of another company, with a different name.

Chapter 1

Born In ATL

T.I. was born in Atlanta, Georgia, on September 25, 1980. His parents named him Clifford Harris, Jr.

Clifford's father was Clifford "Buddy" Harris, Sr. His mother's name was Violeta Morgan. His parents weren't together, though. He lived with his grandparents. They lived in Bankhead. Bankhead is a neighborhood in Atlanta.

Lots of families in Clifford's neighborhood were poor. Growing up, his family didn't have much money.

Clifford loved music, though. He started **rapping** for his family when he was seven years old. A few years later, he was making and recording his own music.

But music didn't keep Clifford out of trouble. Bankhead could be a rough neighborhood. Young people saw they could make money by breaking the law. Many didn't see any other way to earn a living. Selling drugs was dangerous and illegal. People could make money selling drugs, though.

Clifford went to Douglass High School. But he didn't stay long. He ended up dropping out of school. He was selling drugs to make money. He was still making music, though.

If you want to know how successful T.I. is, just ask him. He'll be happy to tell you. He'll also be eager to let you know that he's worked hard to achieve his success.

When he rapped, Clifford used the name Tip. Tip had been his great-grandfather's name.

Moving to Music

In 1998, Tip's cousin introduced him to DJ Toomp from Atlanta. Tip sent DJ Toomp some of his music. The **DJ** liked what he heard.

DJ Toomp liked Tip's music so much that he introduced Tip to Jason Geter. Jason worked for a **recording studio** called Patchwerk Studios. He agreed to become Tip's **manager**. The two still work together today.

Soon, Jason got Tip an **audition** with Kawan "K.P." Prather. K.P. worked for a **label** called LaFace Records. He had his own **imprint**, called Ghet-O-Vision Entertainment. As soon as he heard Tip's music, K.P. signed him to Ghet-O-Vision.

Tip was still a teenager when he signed with Ghet-O-Vision. Tip wanted to make his mark on music. He also wanted to get out of the drug-dealing life. Music was his way to a better life.

Tip Becomes T.I.

Ghet-O-Vision was part of Arista Records. Arista was a big record company. In 2001, Tip moved over to the bigger company. His first album would come out on Arista.

Before Tip's first album came out, he needed to make one change. His name, Tip, was very close to another artist's name. The rapper Q-Tip was also on Arista Records. Out of respect for Q-Tip, Tip changed his name to T.I.

Many people had trouble understanding T.I.'s Southern accent. Some had thought his name was "Chip" because of the way he said "Tip." Now, T.I. wanted to make sure no one got his name wrong. So he spelled it out for everyone, leaving off the last letter.

Tip had become T.I. And T.I. was ready to take on the rap world.

Hip-Hop lingo

A **studio album** is a collection of songs put together in a recording studio.

Producers are the people in charge of putting together songs. A producer makes the big decisions about the music.

A **single** is a song that is sold by itself.

Reggae is a type of music that started in Jamaica. It has a strong beat and combines different types of music, such as blues, jazz, and rock.

The **charts** are lists of the best-selling songs and albums for a week.

When companies **distribute** a work, they advertise it and sell it in many places.

Mixtapes are collections of a few songs put on a CD or given away for free on the Internet without being professionally recorded.

Chapter 2

T.I. Gets Serious

T.I. put out his first **studio album** on October 9, 2001. The album was called *I'm Serious*. *I'm Serious* featured many guest artists. Too Short, Lil Jon, Pharrell Williams, Bone Crusher, and Youngbloodz were all guests on the album.

Several **producers** worked on *I'm Serious*, too. The Neptunes, Brian Kidd, Maseo, and Jazze Pha all produced tracks for the album. T.I. also produced one song, called "Grand Royal." T.I.'s friend DJ Toomp produced six of the album's songs. Finally, Lil Jon produced the remix of "I'm Serious."

The album's only **single** was also called "I'm Serious." The song featured the **reggae** artist Beenie Man. "I'm Serious" didn't get played much on the radio, though. It also didn't make it onto the song **charts**.

I'm Serious didn't get as much attention as T.I. had hoped. Arista Records also wanted T.I.'s album to be a success. They thought they had the next Southern rap star. *I'm Serious* sold around 160,000 copies. That might seem like a lot, but it was much less than T.I. and Arista wanted.

After a slow start with his debut album, T.I.'s second album went gold. That was just the beginning for the up-and-coming hip-hop star. His next album would do even better. It seemed as though there was no stopping this Southern phenomenon.

When *I'm Serious* wasn't a big success, Arista dropped T.I. from the label. Now, he was on his own. He didn't have a record company to get his music out to fans.

Grand Hustle Records

T.I. could have slowed down after Arista dropped him. He wanted to prove he could be successful, though.

In 2003, T.I. started Grand Hustle Records. Jason Geter helped him. They made a deal with Atlantic Records, too. That meant that Grand Hustle's albums could get into more stores around the world. Atlantic Records would help to **distribute** their music for them.

T.I. wanted to get back to where he'd been. He wanted to make more music. He wanted more people to listen to his music.

T.I. started recording **mixtapes** with DJ Drama. T.I. knew he had to spread the word about his music. He had to get people to hear him. The mixtapes helped him get popular.

DJ Drama soon became T.I.'s official DJ. The two played a lot of shows in 2004 and 2005.

Then T.I. was featured on a song by rapper Bone Crusher. The song was called "Never Scared." The video was played on TV. The song was also in the video game *Madden NFL 2004*. The song became popular. It was the first time many people heard T.I. "Never Scared" helped build excitement for T.I.'s next album.

People were starting to recognize T.I.'s name and his sound. They liked his mixtapes. They liked hearing him on Bone Crusher's song. T.I. was on his way to reaching the success he'd missed with *I'm Serious*.

Trap Muzik

T.I. had started Grand Hustle Records. He'd begun building his reputation. Now, T.I. was ready to put out another studio album. This album was called *Trap Muzik*. It was released on August 19, 2003.

Trap Muzik was T.I.'s first album released on his Grand Hustle label. Thanks to the deal Grand Hustle had made with Atlantic, the album had backing from a big company. In many ways, it was the best of both worlds. T.I. and other Grand Hustle artists got to make the music they wanted. But they also had Atlantic's help to put their albums in lots of stores.

Some of the producers who had worked on *I'm Serious* now made beats for *Trap Muzik*. Jazze Pha and DJ Toomp both produced songs for the new album. T.I. also produced a song, just like he did on *I'm Serious*. The song was called "T.I. vs. T.I.P." Producers like Kanye West, David Banner, and San "Chez" Holmes all worked on *Trap Muzik*, too.

Trap Muzik had four main singles. The first was called "24's." Like Bone Crusher's "Never Scared," this song was also in a video game. The game was called *Need for Speed: Underground.* Because of the game, "24's" came out long before *Trap Muzik*. People liked it, and it helped build buzz about the album. "24's" was T.I.'s biggest hit so far.

The next single on the album was called "Be Easy." This song was another big hit. Next, T.I. released "Rubber Band Man." This single did even better than the first two. "Rubber Band Man" reached number 30 on the Hot 100 Singles chart.

By the time Trap Muzik came out, the fans were ready. They'd heard his mixtapes, singles, and guest verses, and they wanted more. In the first week *Trap Muzik* was out, the album sold more than 100,000 copies. The album was the number-four album in the country that week.

In one week, *Trap Muzik* sold nearly as many as *I'm Serious* had sold altogether. Today, *Trap Muzik* has sold more than a million copies.

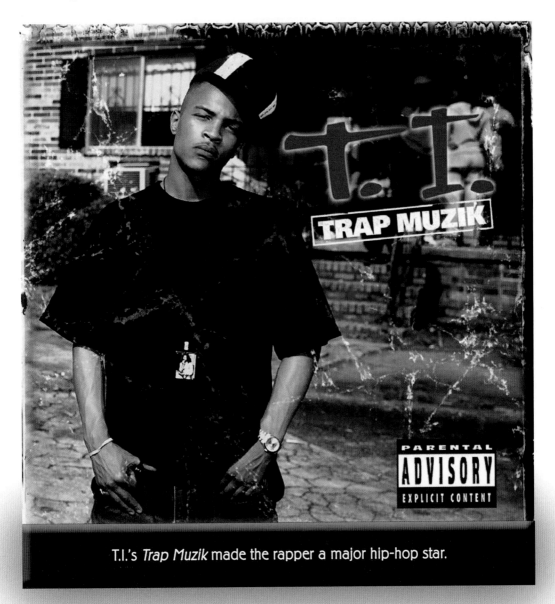

T.I.'s *Trap Muzik* made the rapper a major hip-hop star.

T.I. has dated Tameka "Tiny" Cottle since 2001. Today, the couple is married and have had two children together. Tiny has been with T.I. through good times and bad.

With *Trap Muzik*, T.I. had gone places he'd never been before. His music was more popular than ever. He had more fans than ever. Everything seemed to be going well for the rapper. But T.I. was about to see that everything could end in the blink of an eye.

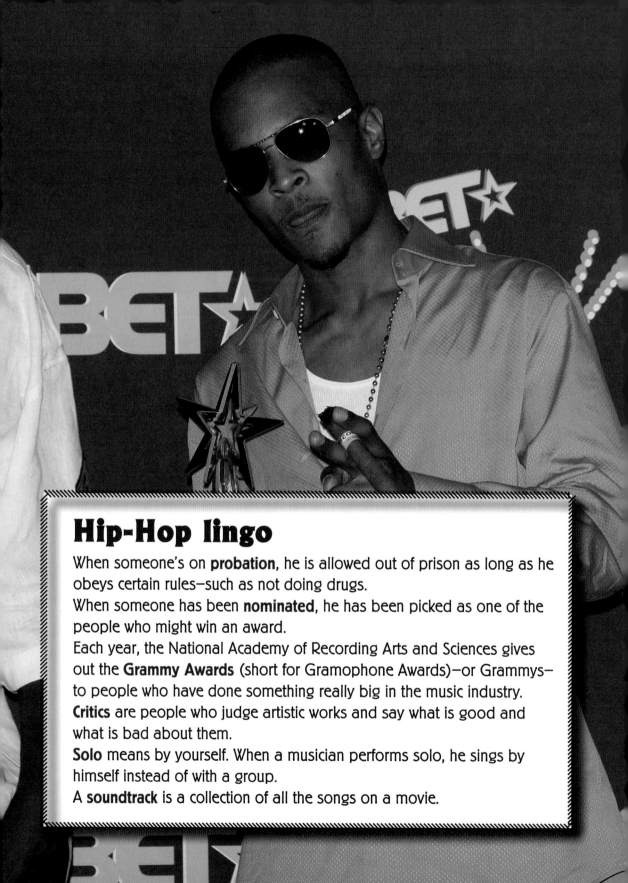

Hip-Hop lingo

When someone's on **probation**, he is allowed out of prison as long as he obeys certain rules—such as not doing drugs.

When someone has been **nominated**, he has been picked as one of the people who might win an award.

Each year, the National Academy of Recording Arts and Sciences gives out the **Grammy Awards** (short for Gramophone Awards)—or Grammys—to people who have done something really big in the music industry.

Critics are people who judge artistic works and say what is good and what is bad about them.

Solo means by yourself. When a musician performs solo, he sings by himself instead of with a group.

A **soundtrack** is a collection of all the songs on a movie.

Chapter 3

T.I. Becomes King

In early 2004, T.I. was arrested for breaking his **probation**. He'd been on probation since 1998, when he was arrested for having drugs. By breaking the rules of his probation, he'd risked his entire music career. He was sentenced to three years in prison.

T.I. started serving his sentence in Cobb County, Georgia. A month after he started his sentence, T.I. got a work release. This meant he could leave prison and work on his music during the day. Then he would go back to prison for the night.

T.I. used his work release to record his next album. He'd almost lost his chance at success. He wasn't going to give up, though.

Urban Legend

On November 30, 2004, T.I. put out his next album. It was called *Urban Legend*.

Urban Legend had many more guest artists than *Trap Muzik*. Nelly, Lil Jon, Lil Wayne, Pharrell Williams, and Lil Kim all rapped on the album.

The first single from *Urban Legend* was called "Bring 'Em Out." Swizz Beatz produced the song. "Bring 'Em Out" was T.I.'s first song to make it into the top ten on the Hot 100 Singles chart. It was T.I.'s biggest hit so far.

The next single, called "U Don't Know Me," wasn't quite as big as "Bring 'Em Out." It was still a hit, though. It helped sell *Urban Legend.* T.I. was getting his songs played on the radio and TV more and more.

Urban Legend sold more than 190,000 copies in the first week it was out. Singles like "Bring 'Em Out" and "U Don't Know Me" helped the album keep selling. Today, it's sold more than a million copies.

The same year that *Urban Legend* came out, T.I. also rapped on a Destiny's Child song. The song was called "Soldier." It also featured Lil Wayne. "Soldier" was very popular. It even reached number three on the Hot 100 Singles chart.

In 2006, T.I. was **nominated** for two **Grammy Awards**. "U Don't Know Me" was up for Best Rap Solo Performance. Destiny's Child's "Soldier" was nominated for Best Song Collaboration.

P$C

T.I. had become a huge rap star in just a few years. He'd gone from being kicked off a major label to starting his own label. He'd gone from not selling enough to selling more than a million.

He didn't lose touch with his home in Atlanta, though. With Grand Hustle Records, he'd been able to stay close to the people and music that helped get him where he was.

T.I. had found another way to stay close to his roots, too. With some friends, he had started a rap group called P$C. The group included AK, Big Kuntry King, C-Rod, and Mac Boney, along with T.I. P$C was first featured on *I'm Serious*. By 2005, the group was on Grand Hustle Records. And they were ready to put out their first album.

In 2005, P$C put out *25 to Life*. The album didn't sell very well. It also got mixed reviews from **critics**. *25 to Life* wasn't a success like T.I.'s **solo** albums. T.I. didn't mind, though. With P$C, he'd been able to stay close with his friends through music.

Urban Legend was another success for T.I. The album's hit singles helped make T.I. one of the most important rappers in hip-hop, and helped him earn the title "King of the South."

Like many recording artists, T.I. wants more than a life in music. For him, that includes films. In this photo, T.I. poses before attending a private screening of his film *ATL*.

King

After *Urban Legend*, T.I. was even more of a star. His song "Bring 'Em Out" became a big hit, bringing him more fans. T.I. was in the spotlight. And he wanted to show everyone that he deserved to be there.

T.I.'s next album was called *King*. *King* was released on March 28, 2006. T.I. had been calling himself the King of the South since *I'm Serious*. After hits like "Bring 'Em Out," many people were saying that T.I. was right.

King featured lots of guest artists. People like Young Jeezy and Jamie Foxx helped on the album.

The first single from *King* was called "What You Know." The song went to number three on the Hot 100 singles charts. "What You Know" was also number one on the Hip-Hop singles chart.

In its first week, *King* sold more than 520,000 copies. It was the number-one album in the country, too. *King* sold more than any other album that week.

King was an important album for T.I. "What You Know" had become a big hit. The album sold very well. But it was also important for another reason.

King came out the same week as a movie called *ATL*. T.I. was starring in *ATL*. It was the first movie T.I. had been in.

ATL and Movies

In *ATL*, T.I. plays Rashad, the main character. *ATL* tells the story of Rashad and his friends growing up in Atlanta. The movie is about trying to follow your dreams when times are tough. T.I. told interviewers that he was excited to work on *ATL*. He said he could relate to the story. T.I. was proud to be helping tell a story about kids in Atlanta. He felt it was a story that didn't always get told.

To costar with Academy Award–winner Denzel Washington (shown here)
was a big "get" for T.I. the actor. T.I. played Denzel's nephew in
American Gangster.

T.I. had also worked on the **soundtrack** for a movie called *Hustle and Flow* in 2005. This movie was about a Southern rapper trying to break into music. With *ATL* and the *Hustle and Flow* soundtrack, T.I. was trying new things.

The weekend *ATL* came out, it made more than 11 million dollars. It was the number-three movie in the country. By the time it left theaters, the movie had made more than 20 million dollars.

King coming out the same week as *ATL* helped sell the album. It also helped sell movie tickets. By having *King* and *ATL* come out in the same week, both sold more than they might have without each other.

The song "What You Know" was also in *ATL*. The song played in commercials for the movie, too. The song became an even bigger hit than it had been when it first came out.

T.I. had always said he was the King of the South. Now he had the huge hit "What You Know," a hit album, and a hit movie. T.I. was looking more and more like a king.

Hip-Hop lingo

When a person is under **house arrest**, he has to stay inside his house and is only allowed certain visitors. House arrest is like being in prison, except it is in your own house.

Consequences are what happen because of something a person has said or done.

Chapter 4

T.I. or T.I.P.?

A little more than a month after *King* and *ATL* came out, T.I. lost his best friend, Philant Johnson. The two men had been friends since they were very young kids. They'd known each other growing up in Atlanta. Johnson and T.I. even went to the same schools together.

When T.I. started moving into music, Johnson helped his friend. Johnson worked as T.I.'s personal assistant. He helped him get from place to place. He kept track of his life when he was busy.

On May 3, 2006, Johnson died. T.I. spoke at Johnson's funeral. He was very sad about losing his friend. He wasn't sure things would ever be the same for him.

When T.I. released the song "Live in the Sky" as a single, he said it was for Philant Johnson. Even though the song was written before Johnson died, T.I. felt it said what he was feeling about losing his friend.

After losing Johnson, T.I. wondered if he would even keep making music. Without his friend, he wasn't sure he wanted to keep rapping.

Collaborations are common in hip-hop, and T.I. has had some of the biggest names appear on his albums. R. Kelly, shown in this photo, was just one of the featured performers on *T.I. vs. T.I.P.*

Cottle, and his kids were the only people allowed to see him. All other visitors needed to go through the courts.

In early 2008, T.I. went to court again. This time, the judge would decide how long T.I. would go to jail. T.I. told the judge he was guilty. He admitted he'd broken the law. The judge said that T.I. had to stay under **house arrest** for a year. He also said that T.I. would have to go to jail. He would have to do some community service, too.

T.I. started his year of house arrest right away. He wasn't allowed to leave except to see the doctor or to go to court. While he was there, he started writing the lyrics for his next album. T.I. wanted to make sure he wasn't wasting any of his time.

Paper Trail

T.I.'s next album was called *Paper Trail*. It came out on September 26, 2008.

The album's name came from T.I.'s new way of working on verses. For the first time since *I'm Serious*, T.I. started writing down his rhymes on paper. For a few albums, he'd just been remembering his lines. Now, he was back to writing things down.

Paper Trail had four successful singles. All four made it into the top five of the Hot 100 singles charts.

The first single was called "Whatever You Like." It came out in August of 2008. By September, the song was number one on the singles charts. The song set the record for largest jump up the chart in one week. It went from 71 to the top spot.

The second single from *Paper Trail* was "Swagga Like Us." The song features Kanye West, Lil Wayne, and Jay-Z. "Swagga Like Us" made it to the fifth spot on the Hot 100 charts. The all-star track was another big hit for T.I.

The next single was called "Live Your Life." This one featured Rhianna. The song broke the record T.I. had set earlier in the year with "Whatever You Like." "Live Your Life" went from number 80 to number one on the singles charts. It was the biggest jump any song had ever made.

The last single from *Paper Trail* was called "Dead and Gone." The song featured Justin Timberlake. T.I. dedicated it to his friend Philant Johnson. The song made it to number two on the Hot 100 singles charts.

Four other songs from the album made it onto the Hot 100 charts, too. Even though these songs weren't released as singles, they were still popular enough to make it onto the charts.

When *Paper Trail* came out, it was the number-one album in the country. In its first week, the album sold 568,000 copies. The album sold more in its first week than T.I.'s other albums had. It was the third album he'd had in a row to come in at number one on the album charts.

At the 2009 Grammys, T.I. performed twice. First, he performed "Swagga Like Us" with Jay-Z, Kanye West, Lil Wayne, and M.I.A. Later, he performed "Dead and Gone" with Justin Timberlake.

That night, T.I. won a Grammy for Best Rap Performance by a Duo or Group for "Swagga Like Us." He was also nominated for other four awards.

Paper Trail was a huge success for T.I. Very few rappers can say they've had four hit songs in one year. But soon, T.I. would have to face the **consequences** of things he'd done in the past.

T.I. Goes to Jail

In March 2009, a judge sentenced T.I. to one year and one day in prison for his 2007 arrest. He also had to pay more than 100,000 dollars for his crime.

T.I. or T.I.P.?

T.I. started his sentence in May of 2009. He was held at a prison in Forrest City, Arkansas.

Before leaving for jail, T.I. held a good-bye concert in Atlanta. The concert was at the Philipps Arena. T.I.'s fans were sad to see the rapper go, even if they knew it was only for a year.

Hip-Hop lingo

A **halfway house** is a home for some people who have gotten out of prison, to help them make the change back to private life.

A **charity** is a group that gives time, money, or other things to help make people's lives better.

Alzheimer's disease is a condition that can develop in old age or middle age. It causes memory loss, personality and mood changes, and loss of mental function. As the disease gets worse, it can also cause loss of physical function, which can lead to death.

Chapter 5

Release and Return

On December 22, 2009, T.I. was let out of prison. He got out before the end of his one-year sentence thanks to his good behavior.

From the Arkansas prison, T.I. was moved to a **halfway house** in Atlanta. He stayed in the halfway house until late March 2010.

The first time T.I. went out after being in jail was to help out his wife's **charity**. Tiny's charity is called "For the Love of Our Fathers." The group helps raise money to find a cure for **Alzheimer's disease**. Both T.I. and Tiny's fathers had had the disease. The charity work means a lot to them. T.I. told people at the event that he was very happy to be out. He even went on stage with Tiny at the end of the event.

After getting out of prison, T.I. also wanted to get back into the music world. He put out a single called "I'm Back" in March of 2010. The song did well. It reached number forty-four on the Hot 100 chart.

T.I. started to do interviews about his time in prison, too. In May, he talked with Larry King on CNN about jail and his music.

Around that time, he put out two more singles. The first song was called "Yeah Ya Know (Takers)." The second was called "Got Your Back." Both songs made it onto the Hot 100 charts.

"Yeah Ya Know (Takers)" was a song from the soundtrack of the movie *Takers*. T.I.'s Grand Hustle Films helped put out the movie in August 2010. The movie is about a group of bank robbers. T.I. acted in *Takers*. He played a character named Ghost. T.I. released "Yeah Ya Know (Takers)" in May to get people excited about the movie.

It seemed like T.I. was on his way back into music after being in prison. But it wasn't long before things took another bad turn.

Return to Prison

On September 1, 2010, T.I. was arrested again. T.I. and his wife, Tiny, were stopped by police in Los Angeles. The police arrested the couple when they found drugs in their car.

The arrest came just a few days after *Takers* opened in theaters. The movie had been a hit. It had reached number one.

In October 2010, T.I. was sentenced to eleven months in jail. He'd been on probation since his 2007 arrest. Now, he'd broken the rules of that probation. T.I. went back to the Forrest City, Arkansas, prison he'd left earlier that year.

No Mercy

T.I. had been working on his next album. He finished the work before he went to jail.

On October 15, 2010, T.I. put out a song from his upcoming album. On the same day, he was sentenced to eleven months in prison. The song was called "Get Back Up." Chris Brown performed on it.

"Get Back Up" was the first taste fans got of T.I.'s new album, *No Mercy*. On December 7, 2010, *No Mercy* was released.

No Mercy featured many guest artists. Kanye West, Kid Cudi, Eminem, The-Dream, Trey Songz, Drake, and Christina Aguilera all performed on the album.

"Get Back Up" was the first single from *No Mercy*. The next single was "Castle Walls." This song featured Christina Aguilera. "Castle Walls" is about how fame and money may seem great, but they can't make you happy.

In one verse of "Castle Walls," T.I. asks how he might feel if his kids end up in the life he had growing up. He asks himself if he'd care about songs or money and things if his kids didn't grow up right.

When *No Mercy* was released, it was at number four on the charts. In the first week, the album sold 159,000 copies. This was much less than T.I.'s recent albums. *No Mercy* was also his first album since *Urban Legend* not to hit number one in its first week.

Looking to the Future

On November 18, 2010, T.I. wrote a letter from prison. He posted it on his website. In it, he told his fans that he's "tired of going to jail." He said that he's been in and out of prison for years. He didn't want to go back ever again.

"Even though it's been a long road, I'm still standing," T.I. wrote.

In August of 2011, T.I. was released from prison. By the end of September, he'd already put out a new single called "I'm Flexin'". He told fans that the song was from his next album. T.I. was already hard at work making music for his fans. And they couldn't have been more excited that the King of the South was back.

Drugs and violence seem to follow T.I. wherever he goes. Despite his
continuing problems, he recognizes that he has reasons to clean up his act.
He owns a company, and many people are affected by his actions.
Most importantly, T.I.'s a father now.

T.I. kept putting out new music throughout 2011. At the end of the year he even put out a free mixtape with all new songs. T.I. told fans that his next album would be called *Trouble Man* and that the album would be out in 2012. In April, 2012, T.I. put out the first single for *Trouble Man*. The song was called "Love This Life."

Music wasn't the only thing keeping T.I. busy after the rapper left prison in 2011. T.I. put out his first novel in October, 2011. The book was called *Power and Beauty: A Love Story of Life on the Streets*.

T.I. also starred in his own reality TV show with his wife, Tiny. The show, *T.I. and Tiny: The Family Hustle*, followed the couple as they raised their children and T.I. gets used to being out of prison again.

T.I.'s been through a lot in the last few years. He's sold millions of albums. He's won important awards for his music. He's acted in movies that have made millions of dollars. But T.I.'s also been in and out of prison a lot.

Now, his fans wait to see what he'll do next. Will T.I. change his life? Will he focus on his music, acting, and other projects? Will he stay away from trouble?

No matter what's next for the King of the South, T.I.'s fans will be waiting. The rapper has had many ups and downs in his time in music, but T.I. is still successful after all he's been through.

1970s   Hip-hop is born in the Bronx, New York.

1973   DJ Kool Herc begins hosting parties in New York.

1979   The Fatback Band produces the first rap record.

1979   Sugarhill Gang's "Rapper's Delight" cracks the Billboard top-10 chart.

September 25, 1980
Clifford Harris—T.I.—is born in Atlanta, Georgia.

1997   T.I. is arrested on drug charges.

1998   T.I.'s cousin introduces him to DJ Toomp.

2000   T.I.'s first child is born, Domani Uriah. He has had six children since then.

2001   T.I. starts dating Tameka "Tiny" Cottle.

2003   T.I. pleads guilty of assaulting a police officer.

2003   T.I. signs with Atlantic Records.

2003   *Trap Muzik* is released.

2004   T.I. turns himself in to authorities on a parole violation.

2004   *Urban Legend* is released.

2005   T.I. co-executive produces the award-winning soundtrack for the film *Hustle & Flow*.

2005   T.I. receives the Lisa Lopes Award for achievement in music and community service.

September 24, 2005
T.I. performs at Boost Mobile's RockCorps concert.

2006   T.I. costars in *ATL*.

2006   *King* is released.

May 3, 2006

T.I. and some of his staff are involved in a shoot-out; his personal assistant is killed.

December 2006

T.I. launches a magazine, *Dapper*.

2007   T.I. is featured in a Chevrolet commercial.

2007   T.I. introduces his own clothing line, A.K.O.O.

2007   T.I. wins two Grammy Awards.

2007   T.I. is arrested again, four hours before the BET Hip-Hop Awards, for possession of unregistered machine guns.

2008   While under house arrest, T.I. starts working on his next album.

2008   T.I. pleads guilty to U.S. federal weapons charges.

2009   Wins Grammy Award for "Swagga Like Us."

2009   Sentenced to one year in prison; fined over $100,000.

February 2010

T.I. makes his first public appearance since prison.

July 30, 2010

T.I. marries "Tiny" in Miami Beach, whom he has two sons with.

September 1, 2010

T.I. and his wife are arrested on drug charges.

October, 2010

T.I. is sentenced to eleven months in prison.

August, 2011

T.I. is released from prison.

September, 2011

T.I. releases "I'm Flexin,'" his first single since leaving prison.

October, 2011

T.I. releases his first novel, *Power and Beauty: A Love Story of Life on the Streets.*

December, 2011

T.I. and Tiny: The Family Hustle premiers on VH1.

April, 2012

T.I. releases the first official single from his eigth album, *Trouble Man.* The song is called "Love This Life."

Discography
Albums

2001   I'm Serious

2003   Trap Muzik

2004   Urban Legend

2006   King

2007   T.I. vs. T.I.P.

2008   Paper Trail

2010   No Mercy

Films

2006   ATL

2007   American Gangster

2008   Once Was Lost

2008   For Sale

2008   Takers

2008   Ballers

Books

Baker, Soren. *The History of Rap and Hip Hop*. San Diego, Calif.: Lucent, 2006.

Comissiong, Solomon W. F. *How Jamal Discovered Hip-Hop Culture*. New York: Xlibris, 2008.

Cornish, Melanie. *The History of Hip Hop*. New York: Crabtree, 2009.

Czekaj, Jef. *Hip and Hop, Don't Stop!* New York: Hyperion, 2010.

Haskins, Jim. *One Nation Under a Groove: Rap Music and Its Roots*. New York: Jump at the Sun, 2000.

Hatch, Thomas. *A History of Hip-Hop: The Roots of Rap*. Portsmouth, N.H.: Red Bricklearning, 2005.

Websites

Grand Hustle
www.grandhustle.com

T.I. Official Website
www.trapmuzik.com

T.I. on the Internet Movie Database
www.imdb.com/name/nm1939267

T.I. on MTV
www.mtv.com/music/artist/t_i_/artist.jhtml

T.I. on MySpace
myspace.com/trapmuzik

Index

Index

About the Author

C.F. Earl is a writer living and working in Binghamton, New York. Earl writes mostly on social and historical topics, including health, the military, and finances. An avid student of the world around him, and particularly fascinated with almost any current issue, C.F. Earl hopes to continue to write for books, websites, and other publications for as long as he is able.

Picture Credits